Trading Basic

Jackson Brooks

Jackson Brooks

Jackson Brooks

Copyright Page

First edition
All Rights Reserved
Author: © 2024, Jackson Brooks

Index

Myths and Truths

The world of trading is full of myths that, in many cases, can lead beginners to enter with completely wrong expectations. These myths not only distort reality, but can also lead many to make wrong decisions from the start. Therefore, it is important to debunk some of the most common myths and compare them with the truth, so that anyone who wants to enter trading does so with a clearer idea of what they can really expect.

One of the most common myths is that to be a good trader you need to be a math genius or have an advanced degree in finance. The reality is very different. While it's true that having financial knowledge can help, the most important skill in trading is not being a number cruncher, but understanding how markets work and, more importantly, how your own emotions work around money. Many successful traders started out with no formal financial experience, but dedicated themselves to learning the basics of technical analysis, chart reading, and managing their emotions when faced with losses or gains. Trading is not an exact science;

it's more of an art in which experience and constant practice play a key role.

Another myth that is commonly heard is that trading is a quick and easy way to get rich. Nothing could be further from the truth. Stories of people making millions of dollars in a short period of time are tempting, but they are often exceptional cases, and the media often ignores the losses that other traders face in the process. Trading requires time, effort, and above all, patience. Most people who start out with the idea of getting rich quick often face great frustrations when things don't go their way. Furthermore, success in trading is not only measured in terms of quick profits, but in consistency over time. Successful traders are not looking to make large amounts of money in a short period of time; they are looking to maintain steady growth and avoid large losses.

It is also common to hear that with trading you can work from anywhere in the world, at any time, and without having to follow a fixed schedule. In part, this is true, as the flexibility of trading is one of its great advantages. You can trade from a laptop or even from your mobile phone, and the markets are open practically around the clock, depending on the type of asset you work with. However, this flexibility comes at a price. Even if you don't have a boss, you must impose rigorous discipline on yourself. It's not like playing a video game where you can enter and leave whenever you want. To be successful, you need to set work schedules, study the markets, analyze your trades, and stay on top of economic news that could affect your investments. In short, trading gives you freedom, but that freedom comes with the need to be responsible and maintain a routine.

Another myth is that you only need one "magic strategy" to make money in trading. It is common for many beginners to look for the perfect formula that will allow them to always win. However, the truth is that there is no strategy that guarantees success in every trade. Financial markets are unpredictable and influenced by many factors, from political changes to global events such as pandemics or natural disasters. Trading strategies must adapt to changing market conditions and what may work today may not work tomorrow. Furthermore, even with a solid strategy, it is impossible to eliminate risk completely. Every trader, no matter how experienced, faces losses at some point. The goal is not to avoid losses completely, but to manage them in a way that does not affect your capital significantly.

Another myth that can be misleading is that you need large amounts of money to start trading. It is true that years ago it was necessary to have a considerable capital to access the financial markets, but today, thanks to digital platforms, it is possible to start with a relatively small investment. However, even if you do not need thousands of dollars to start, it is essential to understand that trading with little capital also has its challenges. When your capital is small, you must be more careful with risk, as a small loss can have a greater impact on your account. The key is to learn to manage risk from the beginning and not get carried away by the idea that you will make a lot of money with little effort just because you started with a small amount.

Finally, there is a myth that only professionals can win at trading, and that beginners are doomed to lose money. This is not entirely true. While it is true that trading is a competitive environment where many lose money, beginners have the opportunity to learn and improve over time. Trading is a skill, and like any skill, it can be developed with practice and study. In addition, there are many educational resources available today, from online tutorials to books and courses, that allow new traders to learn the basics without needing to be experts from the start. The important thing is not to rush, study enough, and start trading in a controlled manner to gain experience without risking all your capital.

In conclusion, trading is an activity that is full of myths and misunderstandings. It is easy to get carried away by the promises of quick money and absolute freedom, but the reality is that success in trading requires discipline, patience and an open mindset to learn from mistakes. You don't need to be a genius or have a lot of money to start, but it is essential to have a realistic attitude and a long-term approach if you want to succeed in this fascinating and challenging world.

Is Trading for Everyone?

Trading is an activity that has captured the attention of many people in recent years, especially with the expansion of digital platforms that make it more accessible than ever. It is common to see advertisements that promise great profits and financial freedom, which generates curiosity and enthusiasm in those looking for an alternative way to generate income. However, an important question arises: is trading really for everyone? The answer, although complex, is that trading is not suitable for everyone, and not because it is an elitist or inaccessible activity, but because it requires a specific set of skills, attitudes and personal characteristics that not everyone possesses or is willing to develop.

For starters, trading demands an ability to handle stress and uncertainty. Unlike other jobs where you have a fixed salary and certain guarantees of stability, trading is an emotional roller coaster. Markets are unpredictable, and price changes can result in huge gains or losses in a matter of minutes. Not everyone is equipped to deal with this level of volatility. Those who are more sensitive to stress or who feel overwhelmed when faced with uncertain situations will likely find trading very difficult to handle. Furthermore, it is easy to get carried away by emotions, whether it is the euphoria of a gain or the fear and frustration of a loss, which can lead to impulsive decisions. In trading, the ability to remain calm and act rationally, even when things are not going as you expect, is an essential skill.

Another important quality is discipline. Trading is not a game of chance where you place your bets and hope that luck does the rest. It is a process that requires careful planning, constant analysis, and above all, following a plan. Successful traders develop clear strategies and stick to them no matter the temptations to stray from the path. This means that you must be disciplined, follow your rules, and avoid making decisions based on hunches or momentary emotions. For many people, this is one of the most difficult parts of trading. In an environment where opportunities seem to arise all the time, it is easy to fall into the trap of overtrading or taking unnecessary risks. If you are not a naturally disciplined person, you might struggle to achieve trading success.

In addition to discipline, trading requires patience. Markets don't always move in the direction you expect, and it can take time before a profitable opportunity appears. Often, novice traders get impatient and want to trade right away, believing that the more trades they make, the more money they'll make. However, the reality is that excessive trading, known as "overtrading," is one of the main reasons why many traders lose money. Being a good trader means patiently waiting for the right moment to act and not getting carried away by the rush. Patience is key to avoiding mistakes and maximizing opportunities, and not everyone has the ability to wait the necessary amount of time without falling into despair or boredom.

Another aspect to consider is risk tolerance. Trading inevitably involves the possibility of losing money. In fact, you will almost certainly lose on a trade at some point, and perhaps lose much more than you expected. For this reason, it is crucial for people who engage in trading to have a mindset that allows them to take risk without fear or anxiety. If you are someone who gets too anxious at the thought of losing money or if you prefer the security of a steady income, trading is probably not the best choice for you. Successful traders understand that losses are part of the game and that the important thing is to manage risk so that a loss does not significantly affect their capital. This type of mindset requires great emotional strength, as the fear of failure or losing money can paralyze you or lead you to make mistakes.

The ability to learn from mistakes is another essential quality for traders. In trading, as in life, not everything always goes as planned, and mistakes are inevitable. What makes the difference between a successful trader and an unsuccessful one is the ability to learn from those mistakes and adapt. Every time you make a mistake, you have the opportunity to analyze what went wrong and improve your approach. However, not all people are willing to accept their failures. There are those who prefer to blame the market, bad luck, or external factors, rather than take responsibility for their decisions. If you are not willing to learn from your mistakes and adjust your strategy, trading can be a very frustrating path.

Another important factor is the availability of time and energy. Although trading can be flexible in terms of schedule, it doesn't mean that it doesn't require dedication. To be a successful trader, you need time to learn, study the markets, analyze charts, and stay on top of news that can influence asset prices. Many people see trading as an activity they can do in their spare time, but the truth is that, at least in the early stages, trading demands a great deal of time to learn and develop the necessary skills. If you are not willing to dedicate the time necessary to learn and improve, it will be difficult for you to achieve consistent results.

Finally, it is important to have adequate capital. Although it is possible to start trading with a small amount of money these days, it is essential that anyone who wants to get involved in trading does not do so with money they cannot afford to lose. Trading involves risk, and it is vital that people are comfortable with the possibility of losing their investment. If you are trading with money that you need to cover your basic expenses, the pressure will be enormous, increasing the likelihood of making impulsive mistakes. Trading with a "can't lose" mentality is a recipe for trading disaster.

In short, trading is not for everyone. Although it is a fascinating and potentially profitable activity, it requires a combination of skills, attitudes and resources that not everyone has or is willing to develop. For those who enjoy challenges, have a tolerance for risk, are patient, disciplined and willing to learn from their mistakes, trading can be an attractive option. However, it is important for each person to assess their own characteristics before diving into this world. The key to success in trading is not in following a magic formula, but in knowing yourself and being prepared to face the challenges that come with this activity.

Curiosities of Trading Throughout History

Trading, although it seems like a modern activity thanks to technology and digital platforms, actually has a fascinating history that dates back centuries. From the first exchanges of goods and products in ancient markets to the complex financial operations of today, trading has been present in one form or another in the lives of human beings. Throughout history, curious and surprising events have occurred that have deeply influenced the way markets operate today. Knowing these historical moments not only allows us to better understand trading, but also learn valuable lessons that apply even in the modern financial world.

One of the earliest examples of trading in history can be found in the ancient civilizations of Mesopotamia, where people practiced barter, exchanging goods such as grain, animals, and precious metals. Barter was an early form of trading, and although it seems very simple compared to what we know today, it laid the groundwork for trade. Over time, people began to use metal coins, such as gold and silver, which made trading much easier and gave rise to the concept of a market. This change allowed traders to begin to specialize, and the idea of making money through price fluctuations gradually emerged.

One of the most curious events in the history of trading is the tulip bubble in Holland during the 17th century. In what is known as the first documented financial bubble, tulips, which were a novelty in Europe, became an object of extreme speculation. People began paying exorbitant sums for tulip bulbs, and the price of these flowers rose dramatically. Some bulbs cost as much as a house, which seems incredible today. However, as with all bubbles, tulip prices fell sharply, and many people who had invested large sums of money in these bulbs lost their fortunes. This event teaches us an important lesson about irrational speculation and how emotion and greed can inflate asset prices beyond their true value.

An equally interesting event occurred in the 18th century, with the creation of the London Stock Exchange. Before formal stock exchanges existed, traders would meet in coffee houses to trade stocks and bonds. One of the most popular coffee houses for doing business was Jonathan's Coffee House in London, which eventually became the meeting point for traders, leading to the formation of the London Stock Exchange. This is a curious fact, as it demonstrates how the foundations of one of the world's most important financial centers grew out of a simple coffee house. Over time, stock exchanges became formalized and began to be regulated, allowing more people to participate in the financial markets.

Another curious moment in trading history is the famous story of Jesse Livermore, an American trader who lived in the early 20th century and is remembered as one of the most daring and successful traders in history. Livermore was known for his ability to predict market movements, and he made large sums of money speculating during times of crisis, such as the Panic of 1907 and the Crash of 1929. In the Crash of 1929, when the New York Stock Exchange collapsed and marked the beginning of the Great Depression, Livermore stood out for selling short and making around $100 million, a huge sum for the time. However, despite his success, Livermore's life was marked by ups and downs, and he ended up losing his fortune several times. His story reminds us that trading can be extremely volatile and that fortunes can be made and lost in a matter of days.

The introduction of computers and digital technology in the second half of the 20th century changed trading forever. Before electronic platforms existed, traders would often place their trades in "pits," which were areas of stock exchanges where traders would shout out their buy and sell orders. This system, known as "outcry trading," was chaotic and depended on how quickly traders could place their bids. However, with the advent of computers, financial markets became much more efficient and accessible. The first exchange to use an electronic platform was the NASDAQ in 1971, and this allowed traders to place their trades more quickly and accurately, without having to be physically present at the stock exchange. This marked the beginning of what we know today as online trading, where anyone with a computer and an internet connection can access global markets.

As trading became more accessible, new forms of speculation also emerged, such as high-frequency trading. This type of trading, which relies on algorithms and ultra-fast computers, makes thousands of transactions per second to take advantage of small movements in prices. Although high-frequency trading has generated huge profits for some companies, it has also been controversial, as many believe that this type of trading creates an unfair advantage for big players and increases volatility in the markets. An example of this was the "Flash Crash" of 2010, when the US market fell sharply in a matter of minutes, only to recover shortly after. This event was largely attributed to algorithmic trading and sparked a discussion about the role of technology in financial markets.

Today, trading has continued to evolve with the rise of cryptocurrencies. Bitcoin, launched in 2009, was the first cryptocurrency to gain global attention, and thousands of other cryptocurrencies have since emerged and are traded on decentralized exchanges. Cryptocurrency trading is a completely new form of speculation, as these assets are not controlled by governments or central banks and their prices can be extremely volatile. Throughout the short history of cryptocurrencies, we have seen huge rises and falls in prices, creating both huge fortunes and huge losses. The funny thing is that even though cryptocurrencies are a relatively new phenomenon, the emotions surrounding them, such as euphoria and fear, are the same ones we have seen in traditional financial markets throughout history.

In short, the history of trading is full of curious and fascinating moments that have shaped the way markets operate today. From bartering in ancient civilizations to algorithmic trading and cryptocurrencies, trading has evolved in surprising ways, but the fundamental principles remain the same: speculation, risk, excitement, and above all, the quest to take advantage of price fluctuations to make a profit. These historical events not only show us how trading has changed, but they also teach us valuable lessons about the dangers of irrational speculation and the importance of having a solid strategy in the markets.

How Does It Affect Your Trading Decisions?

The decisions you make in trading are influenced by many factors, and some of them are not always obvious. In the world of trading, every decision can make a huge difference between making or losing money, and while we all try to make rational and well-informed choices, the truth is that our emotions, past experiences, and beliefs play a crucial role in how we act. When we talk about how something affects our trading decisions, it is important to recognize that it is not just about data, charts, or technical analysis. Sometimes, personal or psychological factors can have a bigger influence than we imagine.

One of the factors that most affects trading decisions is fear. Fear is a powerful emotion that can cloud our judgment and cause us to make impulsive decisions. In trading, fear often appears when we are faced with the possibility of losing money. This fear of losses can be paralyzing, causing you to avoid taking risks or sell too quickly, missing out on opportunities for greater profits. Instead of following a plan or strategy you have prepared, fear makes you react defensively. Maybe you have had a bad experience in the past, such as a big loss, and that stays in your mind every time you enter a new trade. Fear, in many cases, makes you doubt your decisions, even when your analysis is correct, and this can lead to mistakes that could have been avoided.

Another factor that greatly influences trading decisions is greed. We all want to make money, and it's normal to want to make the most of every opportunity, but when greed takes over, it can blind you to the risks. Greed makes you think that you can always make a little more, that the market will continue to rise or fall in your favor, and leads you to risk more than necessary. Often, traders who let greed guide their decisions don't know when to stop. They hold their positions open for too long, hoping for bigger and bigger profits, until the market turns around and they end up losing what they've already made. Greed makes you forget the importance of having a plan and taking profits at the right time.

Besides emotions, our past experiences also play a major role in how we make trading decisions. If you have been successful on a recent trade, you are likely to feel more confident about your next decisions. This confidence is good, but it can sometimes lead you to take unnecessary risks. You think that because you were successful on the last trade, you will be successful on the next one, not realizing that every trade is unique and that market conditions change. On the other hand, if you had a bad experience, you may become more cautious or even too reluctant to take risks, which can also limit your chances of success. What this teaches us is that our trading decisions are not always based only on the present, but are also conditioned by our past experiences, both good and bad.

Lack of patience is another factor that affects many trading decisions. Sometimes traders rush into or out of the market simply because they don't want to wait. Maybe you see the market moving quickly and feel like if you don't act right away, you'll miss out on an opportunity. However, this lack of patience can lead you to make rash decisions. Maybe you enter a trade before a clear signal is confirmed, or maybe you exit early out of fear that the market will turn. Impatience can be especially dangerous in trading because it leads you to trade more than necessary, which increases the chances of making mistakes. Successful trading requires waiting for the right moment to act, and lack of patience is one of the reasons why many traders lose money.

Another aspect that influences trading decisions is peer pressure or the influence of others. We live in an age where information is instantly available, and in the trading world, it's easy to be influenced by what others are doing. You might see on social media or trading forums that many people are buying or selling a particular asset, and you're tempted to go with the flow. This peer pressure can lead you to make decisions that aren't aligned with your own analysis or strategy. Instead of acting based on your plan, you may fall into the trap of doing what everyone else is doing for fear of being left out. This is known as the "herd effect," and it's one of the most common mistakes in trading. Following the crowd is rarely a good idea, as markets are unpredictable and what works for others won't always work for you.

We should also talk about the importance of self-control in trading. Self-control is the ability to stick to your decisions, even when emotions try to influence you. However, many times this self-control is undermined by the pressure of wanting to make money quickly. Instead of sticking to your strategy and having the patience to wait for the best opportunities, you may be tempted to trade too often, simply because you don't want to miss out on any opportunities. This constant desire to be trading can erode your self-control and lead you to make mistakes. Self-control is essential in trading because it helps you stay focused on your long-term goals and avoid impulsive decisions.

Unrealistic expectations also greatly affect trading decisions. Many people enter the world of trading with the hope of getting rich quick, but the reality is that trading is not a quick way to make money. It's easy to be fooled by success stories of traders who have made millions, but those stories are often the exception rather than the rule. Having expectations that are too high can cause you to make unwise decisions, such as taking unnecessary risks or trading more frequently than you should. If you think that every trade will lead to big profits, you'll likely end up making decisions that aren't based on sound analysis. The most important thing is to keep realistic expectations and remember that trading is a long-term process that requires time and patience.

In addition to emotions and expectations, the amount of information we are exposed to also affects our decisions. In the trading world, there is information overload. Every day, we receive news, analysis, expert opinions, and even rumors that can influence our thoughts and decisions. Sometimes, the amount of information can be overwhelming and lead to "paralysis by analysis," where you feel like you can't make a decision because there are too many factors to consider. Other times, you may make hasty decisions based on a single piece of information that seems important at the time, but in reality doesn't carry that much weight.

Learning to filter information and focus on what really matters is crucial to making better trading decisions.

Finally, it is important to recognize that the environment you are in also affects your trading decisions. If you are trading in a place where there is a lot of noise or distractions, you are more likely to make impulsive decisions. Trading requires concentration and a quiet environment in order to analyze the market clearly. If you do not have a proper trading space or if you are constantly interrupted, it will be more difficult to make informed decisions. In addition, your physical and mental state also influences your decisions. If you are tired, stressed, or emotionally drained, you are more likely to make mistakes. Therefore, it is essential that you take care of your overall well-being, both physically and mentally, in order to make better decisions.

In conclusion, trading decisions are influenced by a combination of emotions, past experiences, expectations, and the environment in which you operate. Fear, greed, impatience, social pressure, lack of self-control, unrealistic expectations, and information overload can negatively affect your decisions if you are not aware of their impact. Therefore, it is essential that every trader learns to identify these factors and manage them effectively. Only then will you be able to make more informed and consistent trading decisions, avoiding the mistakes that many traders make when they let their emotions and external circumstances influence their choices.

What You Should Know

Before you start trading in the financial markets, there are several important things you need to know. Trading may seem like an exciting way to make money, and in some cases it is, but it is also full of risks and challenges. To be successful, it is not enough to learn how to read charts or follow market news – you need to have a deep understanding of how markets work, what factors affect asset prices, and most importantly, how to control your emotions and stay calm in times of high pressure. In this chapter, we are going to explore what you really need to know before you enter the world of trading, so that you can make more informed decisions and avoid common mistakes.

The first thing you need to know is that trading is not a quick and easy way to get rich. Although you sometimes hear stories of traders who made a fortune in a short period of time, those cases are the exception, not the rule. Most successful traders have spent years learning, practicing, and honing their skills. Trading is a career like any other: it requires time, dedication, and effort. Don't expect to make huge profits overnight, and be wary of unrealistic expectations. While it is possible to make money in trading, it is also possible to lose money, and there are no guarantees of success. Most importantly, don't view trading as a lottery or a game of chance, but rather as a process in which you make decisions based on analysis and planning.

Another crucial point is that the market is unpredictable. Many beginners think that if they can learn to read charts well or follow financial news, they will be able to anticipate exactly what the market will do. However, the reality is that no matter how much analysis you do, there will always be unexpected factors that affect the price of assets. Sometimes, markets will move in directions contrary to what logic or analysis suggests, and that can be frustrating. It is important to understand that you do not have control over the market. The only thing you can control is how you react to market movements. This means that you must be prepared to accept losses when things do not go your way, and not try to force the market to move in your favor. Instead, you must have a flexible mindset and be willing to adapt to changing conditions.

It is also essential that you understand the concept of risk. Every time you make a trade, you are taking a risk. Even the safest-looking trade can result in a loss. That is why one of the basic principles of trading is to learn how to manage risk. This means that you should never risk more than you are willing to lose on a single trade. Many beginner traders make the mistake of betting large amounts of money on a single trade because they are sure that they will make a profit, but if that trade results in a loss, they can lose a significant portion of their capital. Risk management involves setting clear limits on how much you are willing to lose on each trade and sticking to those limits, regardless of what happens in the market. In this way, you protect your capital and ensure that a single trade does not jeopardize your entire portfolio.

One of the most important skills you need to develop as a trader is the ability to control your emotions. In trading, emotions play a much bigger role than people realize. Fear and greed are two of the emotions that most affect traders' decisions. When the market is against you, it's easy to get carried away by fear and make impulsive decisions, such as closing a trade too early to avoid a bigger loss. On the other hand, when you're making money, greed can lead you to hold a trade open for longer than you should, hoping to make even more, only to see the market turn around and you lose everything you've made. Controlling these emotions is key to making rational decisions and not letting your feelings cloud your judgment.

It is important to have a trading plan before you enter the market. Many people make the mistake of starting to trade without a clear strategy. Trading without a plan is like sailing a ship without a compass; you have no clear direction and are at the mercy of the winds and waves. A trading plan should include your objectives, the conditions under which you will enter and exit the market, how you will manage risk, and how you will handle your emotions. This plan will serve as a guide for you to make consistent decisions and not let panic or euphoria lead you to make impulsive decisions. A good trading plan will help you maintain discipline and follow a logical strategy, rather than reacting to every market move.

One thing you should also know is that trading takes time. Many people think they can trade the markets by spending just a few minutes a day, but the reality is that trading requires a lot of attention and analysis. You have to keep up with the news, follow market movements, and constantly analyze your trades. While there are ways to automate some parts of the process, such as using stop losses or algorithmic trading, you will still need to spend time studying the market and improving your trading skills. In the long run, the more time you invest in learning and practicing, the more likely you are to succeed.

Another aspect that many people overlook is the importance of continuing education in trading. Financial markets are constantly changing, and what works today may not work tomorrow. That's why it's critical that you're always learning and updating your knowledge. This includes studying new strategies, learning from your mistakes, and staying on top of trends and technologies that affect the market. Continuing education is what separates successful traders from those who fail. Don't settle for what you already know; always seek to improve and learn more.

Finally, one of the most important things to know is that not every day will be a good day. There will be days when the market doesn't move the way you expected, when your strategies don't work, and when you lose money. This is part of trading, and it's something you need to accept from the start. Success in trading isn't measured by a single trade, but by consistency over time. Even the most experienced traders have bad days, but what sets them apart is their ability to bounce back from losses and keep moving forward. If you can learn to accept losses and not be discouraged by them, you'll be on the right path to trading success.

In conclusion, before you start trading, it is essential that you understand that trading is not easy, nor fast, nor a guarantee of success. You must be prepared to face challenges, manage risk, control your emotions, and spend time improving your skills. Trading requires patience, discipline, and a solid plan. If you can approach trading with a realistic mindset and be willing to learn from your mistakes, you will be better prepared to face market uncertainties and increase your chances of success.

Cases of Traders Who Lost

The trading world is full of success stories, but it is also full of cases of traders who, despite their experience, knowledge or confidence, have lost large amounts of money. These stories are not only lessons for beginners, but they also remind us how important risk management, discipline and humility are in the markets. Throughout history, we have seen cases of traders who, due to mistakes, bad decisions or unexpected factors, have faced devastating losses. In this chapter, we are going to explore some of those cases, not with the aim of discouraging you, but so that you can learn from their mistakes and better understand the risks involved in trading.

One of the most famous cases is that of Nick Leeson, a trader who worked for Barings bank in the 1990s. Leeson started out as a successful trader on the Singapore Stock Exchange, but over time he began taking excessive risks and making ever larger bets on the futures market. When the market began to move against him, instead of cutting his losses, Leeson tried to recoup the money he lost by increasing his bets, which only made matters worse. In the end, his trades caused losses of over $1 billion, leading to the bankruptcy of Barings, one of England's oldest banks. This case is a reminder that no matter how experienced you are, if you don't manage risk properly, losses can quickly grow out of control.

Another significant case is that of Jerome Kerviel, a trader at the French bank Société Générale. Kerviel was known for taking huge risks in his trades, and for a time, his strategies brought him huge profits. However, as is often the case in trading, things did not go as he expected. Kerviel began to make increasingly risky decisions, hiding his losses from the bank's management. As his bets failed, the losses piled up until, in 2008, the bank discovered that it had lost more than €6 billion. This case shows how, when a trader lets himself be carried away by greed and loses sight of reality, he can end up in disastrous situations, not only for himself, but also for the institution he works for.

There is also the case of Bill Hwang, a hedge fund manager who, in 2021, was caught up in one of the biggest financial collapses in recent history. Hwang ran a fund called Archegos Capital, and for years he had been successful using leveraged trading strategies – trading with borrowed money to boost his profits. However, when some of his biggest bets on tech stocks started to fail, his positions quickly collapsed, and because of the high level of leverage he had used, the losses were massive. Within days, Archegos lost more than $20 billion, and the fund's collapse affected several major banks that had funded its trades. This case illustrates the dangers of leverage and how, when markets move against you, the losses can be much larger than you had anticipated.

An example that also deserves attention is that of Long-Term Capital Management (LTCM), an investment fund created by some of the world's most respected economists, including two Nobel Prize winners. LTCM used arbitrage strategies and advanced mathematical models to make highly leveraged trades. For the first few years, the fund was incredibly successful, generating huge returns for its investors. However, in 1998, when the financial crisis in Russia occurred, global markets began to behave unpredictably, and LTCM's mathematical models were unable to anticipate these movements. The fund suffered massive losses in a short time, and due to the extreme leverage they used, the losses jeopardized the stability of several large banks. In the end, the US government had to intervene to prevent a major financial collapse. This case shows that even the smartest traders and economists can be wrong, and that mathematical models cannot always predict market behavior.

Another well-known case is that of Victor Niederhoffer, a famous fund manager who for years was considered one of the best traders in the world. Niederhoffer had built a solid reputation as a successful trader in the futures and options markets, and had generated large profits for his clients. However, in 1997, during the Asian financial crisis, Niederhoffer underestimated the impact of volatility on the markets and held positions that were too risky. When the market moved sharply against him, the losses were so great that his fund went bust, and he lost much of his personal fortune. Despite being considered a trading genius,

Niederhoffer fell into the trap of not properly managing risk, and his story is an important lesson in how arrogance and overconfidence can lead to failure.

Even independent traders, those who trade on their own without working for large banks or hedge funds, have also faced devastating losses. One example is that of many traders who participated in the tech bubble of the late 1990s. During that time, tech stocks were soaring, and many traders began trading based on market euphoria, thinking that prices would continue to rise indefinitely. However, when the bubble burst in 2000, tech stocks fell dramatically, and many of those traders, who had not protected their investments, lost large amounts of money. This case is a reminder that markets can be extremely volatile, and that it is important not to get carried away by the emotion of the moment.

There are also more familiar cases, such as that of traders who were affected by the cryptocurrency market crisis. In 2021 and 2022, many traders were attracted by the promise of huge profits in the cryptocurrency market. During that time, the prices of cryptocurrencies, such as Bitcoin and Ethereum, reached all-time highs, and many traders, both experienced and novice, invested large sums of money. However, in 2022, cryptocurrency prices suddenly plummeted, and those who had not diversified their investments or managed their risk well suffered considerable losses. This case is a lesson in the importance of being cautious in extremely volatile markets, such as the cryptocurrency market, and not investing more than you can afford to lose.

These examples of traders who lost large amounts of money have one thing in common: in many cases, the losses were the result of not properly managing risk, letting emotions guide decisions, or underestimating market volatility. Even the most experienced traders can make these mistakes, and that is why it is crucial that, as a trader, you always stay disciplined, stick to your trading plan, and never give in to euphoria or panic. Trading is a high-risk activity, and while profits can be tempting, you should always remember that every trade carries the possibility of loss. Learning from other traders' mistakes is one of the best ways to avoid making the same mistakes yourself.

In conclusion, the cases of traders who have lost large sums of money show us that success in trading is not guaranteed, and that even the most intelligent or experienced can face major failures if they do not manage risk correctly or if they allow emotions to cloud their judgment. It is important to study these cases, learn from them, and above all, remember that trading requires discipline, patience, and a rational approach. If you can avoid the mistakes that others have made, you will be better prepared to face the challenges of the market and increase your chances of success.

Stress and Mental Health

Trading, at first glance, may seem like an exciting activity full of opportunities to generate profits. However, what many do not consider at first is the impact it can have on the mental health of those who practice it. Stress is a constant in trading, due to the unpredictable and fast-moving nature of the markets. This stress, if not managed correctly, can affect both the emotional and physical well-being of a person, and in some cases, lead to situations of extreme exhaustion. In this chapter, we are going to talk about how trading-related stress can influence your mental health, what factors cause it, and most importantly, how to manage it effectively.

One of the main reasons why trading is so stressful is because it involves money. Every trade you make is directly related to your capital, and knowing that you can make or lose money in a matter of minutes can create a lot of pressure. This constant feeling of uncertainty can lead to anxiety, especially if you're inexperienced or if you're on a losing streak. When the markets are moving against you, it's easy to fall into a cycle of negative thoughts, worrying about every move and fearing that every decision you make will be the wrong one. This type of psychological pressure can lead to mental overload if you don't know how to deal with it.

Another factor that contributes to stress in trading is the fact that many times the results are not in your hands. Even if you do a perfect analysis, the market can react unpredictably to external factors that you cannot control. Economic news, political events, or even rumors can make the market move in unexpected directions. This can make you feel helpless, as no matter how much effort you put into your analysis, there will always be an element of uncertainty that you cannot eliminate. That lack of control is a constant source of stress, and if you do not know how to manage it, it can affect your emotional well-being in the long run.

Trading stress can also take a toll on your physical health. Many traders spend long hours in front of a screen, analyzing charts, following news, and making snap decisions. This lack of rest can lead to sleep problems, exhaustion, and fatigue. In addition, prolonged stress can trigger physical problems such as headaches, muscle tension, and even digestive problems. In the long term, chronic stress can have a negative impact on your immune system, making you more vulnerable to illness. That's why it's essential that as a trader you learn to take care of both your mind and your body, as the two are closely related.

One of the biggest threats to traders' mental health is the constant pressure to succeed. In the trading world, success is celebrated and failure is punished. This can lead many traders to set unrealistic expectations for themselves, hoping to make huge profits quickly. When things don't go their way, it's easy to fall into frustration and self-criticism. This constant pressure to win and avoid losing can leave you feeling unmotivated and anxious, which directly affects your ability to make logical decisions. If you don't know how to handle the pressure, you may start trading on impulse, often resulting in even bigger losses.

Isolation is another factor that affects traders' mental health. Unlike other jobs, trading is an activity that many people do independently, from home or in private offices. This isolation can lead to feelings of loneliness, especially if you don't have a support network with whom you can share your experiences. Without someone to talk to or vent to, stress can build up and leave you feeling overwhelmed. Sharing your challenges and frustrations with other traders or friends can be an effective way to relieve stress and maintain a balanced perspective.

The lack of structure in a trader's daily life can also be a source of stress. Unlike more traditional jobs, where there are set hours and established routines, trading is an activity that requires flexibility and adaptability. This means that traders often work irregular hours, depending on the markets they trade. The lack of a set schedule can cause some traders to neglect self-care, such as exercise, healthy eating, or adequate rest. It is essential that you establish a daily routine that allows you to balance the time you spend trading with other activities that help you maintain your physical and mental well-being.

The competitive nature of trading can also take a toll on your mental health. You're constantly comparing yourself to other traders, seeing their successes, and wondering why you're not getting the same results. This constant comparison can lead to feelings of inferiority or frustration, especially when you see others achieving their goals while you're dealing with losses. It's important to remember that trading is an individual experience, and every trader has their own pace of learning and growth. Comparing yourself to others not only distracts you from your own goals, but it can also increase the stress and pressure you feel to succeed.

To manage stress in trading, the first thing you need to do is accept that losses are part of the process. No matter how good you are or how long you've been trading, there will be times when you lose money. The important thing is to not let those losses affect your confidence or lead you to make impulsive decisions. The key is to learn from your mistakes and view each loss as an opportunity to improve. Additionally, setting realistic expectations about your wins and losses will help reduce the pressure you feel to succeed on every trade.

Self-care also plays a crucial role in stress management. Make sure you take regular breaks during the day and don't spend endless hours in front of a screen. Regular exercise, a balanced diet, and getting enough sleep are all key to keeping your body and mind in good shape. It's also important to find activities outside of trading that help you unwind and relax. Whether it's playing a sport, reading a book, or spending time with friends and family, having a balanced life outside of the market is essential to maintaining good mental health.

Another effective strategy for managing stress is meditation and mindfulness. Meditation helps you calm your mind and reduce anxiety levels, allowing you to make more rational and less impulsive decisions. Practicing mindfulness also teaches you to be present in the moment, rather than worrying about the future or what could go wrong. This technique is especially useful in trading, where the pressure to anticipate market movements can be overwhelming.

Finally, it's important to seek support when you need it. Talking to other traders or a mental health professional can help you put your challenges into perspective and find effective ways to deal with stress. You don't have to face trading challenges alone, and recognizing when you need help is a sign of strength, not weakness.

In short, stress and mental health are key aspects of trading that should not be ignored. Trading can be an intense and demanding activity, but with the right tools, you can learn to manage stress effectively and protect your mental and physical well-being. Remember that success in trading is not just about making money, but also about maintaining a healthy balance in your life. By taking care of your mental health, you will be better prepared to face market challenges and make clearer and more effective decisions.

What Makes a Successful Trader?

What makes a successful trader? That is the question that many people ask themselves when they start to delve into the world of trading. It is easy to think that success in this field depends solely on making money or making perfect trades all the time. But the reality is much more complex than that. Success in trading is not defined by profits alone, but by a combination of skills, mindset, discipline, and the ability to constantly learn. To be successful, it is not enough to know when to buy and when to sell. There are several important factors that determine whether someone can become a successful trader in the long run.

The first thing that distinguishes a successful trader is his mindset. The way a trader thinks and approaches the market is key to his success. A successful trader does not get carried away by emotions or allow fear or greed to control his decisions. Staying calm and objective is essential, especially when markets become volatile. If a trader acts impulsively out of fear of losing or a desire for quick profits, he is likely to make costly mistakes. Success in trading depends largely on having the ability to make rational decisions, based on data and analysis, not passing emotions.

Another key trait of a successful trader is discipline. Trading can be tempting because it seems to offer the chance to make money quickly, but it is actually a long-term game. Successful traders are those who follow their strategies consistently and in a disciplined manner. This means that they do not deviate from their plan when things do not go their way. For example, if a trader has decided that they are only going to invest in certain assets or that they are going to use a specific strategy, they should not change course just because the market is suddenly going up or down. Discipline also involves being patient, waiting for the right time to enter and exit the market, rather than trying to rush things for fear of missing an opportunity.

The ability to learn and adapt is another key component of trading success. Markets are constantly changing, and what worked yesterday may not work tomorrow. A successful trader knows that he or she must always be learning and improving. This means being willing to acknowledge one's mistakes and learn from them. Successful traders don't view losses as failures, but rather as lessons that can help them improve. They are constantly seeking new information, whether through books, courses, or simply by analyzing their own trades. They also know how to adapt to changing market conditions. This doesn't mean that they change their strategy every time the market moves, but rather that they adjust their approach based on new circumstances.

Risk management is another essential quality of a successful trader. Many beginner traders make the mistake of focusing only on how much they can win, without considering how much they could lose. A successful trader, on the other hand, always takes into account the risk of each trade before making a decision. He sets clear limits on how much he is willing to lose on a trade and follows those rules to the letter. No matter how promising an opportunity seems, a disciplined trader never risks more than he can afford to lose. This risk management is what allows a trader to stay in the game for the long haul, even when facing losses.

Perseverance is another important trait. Trading is a journey full of ups and downs. There will be days when you win and days when you lose, and it's easy to feel demotivated when things don't go your way. However, a successful trader is someone who doesn't give up easily. They understand that success doesn't come overnight and that every setback is an opportunity to improve. Perseverance doesn't mean trading more when things go wrong, but rather having the ability to keep learning, adjusting strategies, and moving forward despite the difficulties. This is one of the reasons why many beginning traders don't become successful – they don't have the patience or fortitude to get through the tough times.

Emotional control also plays a crucial role in a trader's success. The market can be unpredictable, and sometimes sudden movements can create fear or euphoria. Successful traders know how to keep their emotions in check. They don't let a series of winning trades make them feel invincible, or a losing streak plunge them into despair. Maintaining emotional balance is essential to making objective decisions and avoiding impulsive behavior that can lead to losses. Successful traders know that strong emotions, whether positive or negative, can cloud their judgment and cause them to lose sight of their strategy and long-term goals.

Planning is also key. A successful trader doesn't enter the market without a clear plan. They know exactly what they're looking for in a trade, how much they're willing to risk, and when they plan to exit. Having a plan and sticking to it is essential to avoid making hasty or impulsive decisions. Additionally, a good trading plan not only includes strategies for when to buy and sell, but also clear rules for money management and risk management. Successful traders also review and adjust their plans regularly to ensure they're aligned with current market conditions and their own goals.

Finally, a successful trader understands that success is not measured by profits alone. While making money is the ultimate goal of trading, a truly successful trader measures their success in terms of consistency and progress. This means being able to consistently generate profits, but also continually improving their ability to manage risk, control their emotions, and follow their plan in a disciplined manner. Long-term success in trading is not a matter of making a big profit once in a while, but rather being able to stay in the market for years, riding out the ups and downs and always improving.

In short, what makes a successful trader is not just the ability to make money, but a combination of mindset, discipline, technical skills, and the ability to learn and adapt. Traders who achieve success are those who are willing to put in the effort to constantly improve, who have a long-term vision, and who know how to manage risk effectively. While the path of trading is full of challenges, those who manage to master these qualities can find not only financial success, but also great personal satisfaction in their ability to navigate the markets in an intelligent and balanced manner.

The Power of Discipline and Patience in Trading

Discipline and patience are two of the most important pillars in the world of trading. Anyone who wants to be successful in this activity must understand that trading is not just about making quick and risky decisions, but about knowing when to act and when to wait. These concepts, although simple, are difficult to master because they involve controlling emotions and impulses, two things that often strongly influence the decisions of those who are starting out in trading. Throughout this chapter, we are going to explore how discipline and patience can make the difference between success and failure in trading.

Let's start by talking about discipline. In trading, discipline is what allows you to follow your plan consistently, no matter what is happening in the market. A disciplined trader knows that he cannot make decisions based on impulse or emotion, but must act according to his analysis and strategy. This means that before entering the market, the trader has already set clear rules about when to buy, when to sell, how much to risk, and what his profit target will be. It is not about trading on instinct, but rather following a plan that has been developed with time and care. Discipline is what stops you from doing things you know you shouldn't do, such as entering a trade just because the market seems to be moving fast, or staying in a trade that is clearly going against you in the hope that it will reverse.

A common mistake among beginner traders is a lack of discipline. When they see that the market is moving quickly, they feel the need to act immediately, even if they haven't done a proper analysis. This is what is called "impulsive trading," and it is one of the main reasons why many traders end up losing money. The market is always going to move, but that doesn't mean you should participate in every move. A disciplined trader knows how to wait for the right moment to enter, and if they don't find a good opportunity, they are able to stay out. There is no worse mistake in trading than acting without a clear reason.

Patience goes hand in hand with discipline. In trading, you're not always going to get immediate results, and this is where the real power of patience comes in. Impatient traders often make the mistake of jumping in and out of the market quickly, looking to make immediate profits. However, the market doesn't always move in the direction you expect right away, and you may have to wait a while before you see the results of your trade. Patience allows you to stay calm and not close a trade prematurely just because you don't see quick profits.

Patience is also crucial when things aren't going your way. Not every trade is going to be a winner, and sometimes the market will move against you. An impatient trader may get frustrated and abandon his strategy when faced with a losing streak, but a patient trader knows that losses are part of the process. There isn't a trader in the world who hasn't had losses, and it is precisely patience that has allowed them to keep going and eventually recover what they lost. Patience helps you keep a long-term view, understanding that trading is not a short-term game, but an activity in which real results are seen over time.

Another reason why patience is so important in trading is that the market often tests you. You may have an excellent strategy, but if you are not patient, you may get out too early and miss out on the opportunity to maximize your profits. For example, imagine you enter a trade and see the market slowly start to move in your favor. An impatient trader might close the trade immediately to secure a small profit, but a patient trader will wait for the right moment to maximize their profits, following their set plan and goals. Of course, this doesn't mean you should stay in a trade indefinitely, but having patience will allow you to take advantage of bigger opportunities when they present themselves.

Furthermore, patience is necessary to learn and improve at trading. Trading is a complex activity that takes time to master. It is not just about knowing the strategies and technical analysis, but also understanding how the market works and how to respond to different situations. Many beginner traders feel demotivated when they do not get immediate results, and that can lead them to give up too soon. The reality is that learning to be a good trader takes time, and you need to be patient both with the learning process and with yourself. Over time, you will accumulate experience and improve your skills, but this is only possible if you have the patience to keep going despite the initial challenges.

Discipline and patience are also key when it comes to managing risk. A disciplined and patient trader doesn't risk more than he can afford to lose, and he knows that not every opportunity is worth it. Sometimes, it's better not to trade than to risk too much on a trade that doesn't meet your criteria. This is one of the hardest lessons to learn, but it's vital to protecting your capital in the long run. A successful trader doesn't just focus on winning, but also on protecting what he already has. Patience helps you wait for the right opportunity, and discipline ensures that you stick to your plan without deviating.

An interesting aspect of trading is that although the market is fast-paced and volatile, the most successful traders are those who know how to wait. They don't get carried away by the speed of the market, but instead watch it calmly and act only when they see a clear opportunity. This requires a level of self-control that can only be achieved through discipline and patience. Traders who lack these qualities often feel overwhelmed by the pressure of having to constantly act, which can lead them to make hasty and, in many cases, wrong decisions.

In short, the power of discipline and patience in trading should not be underestimated. These are two qualities that, although often overlooked, are critical to long-term success. Discipline helps you stick to your strategy, while patience allows you to wait for the best opportunities and not make hasty decisions. Together, these two qualities will help you maintain control over your emotions, manage risk effectively, and ultimately achieve your goals as a trader. The path to trading success is neither quick nor easy, but with discipline and patience, you will be better prepared to face the challenges and take advantage of the opportunities that the market has to offer.

The Influence of the Environment on Your Financial Decisions

Our environment has a much bigger influence on our financial decisions than we might imagine. Sometimes we think that our money decisions are completely rational and based solely on data and logic. However, the reality is that we are constantly surrounded by external factors that can affect how we manage our finances. This is especially true in the world of trading, where decisions need to be made quickly and accurately, and where the environment you find yourself in can cause you to make very different decisions than you would in a calmer or more controlled context.

One of the most influential factors in our financial decisions is our social environment. The people around us, whether it's our family, friends, coworkers, or even the people we follow on social media, can affect how we view our finances and how we act accordingly. For example, if you're surrounded by people who constantly talk about how they made quick money trading or investing, you're likely to feel pressure to do the same. This pressure can cause you to make rash decisions or take risks you wouldn't normally take. Maybe you see someone on social media bragging about their big wins, and that leads you to want to imitate their behavior, even without having the same knowledge or experience.

Family environment also plays a key role. If you grew up in a home where money was always a source of worry or conflict, those experiences are likely to influence how you handle your finances as an adult. You may feel a constant need to save for fear of running out of money, or you may be more inclined to spend impulsively to avoid the stress you associate with saving. In trading, these influences can manifest in investment decisions that are not aligned with your long-term goals, simply because your environment has shaped you to act a certain way regarding money.

The economic environment and news also have a huge impact on our financial decisions. Every day we are bombarded with information about the global economy, financial markets, and expert predictions. If the news is positive, such as that the markets are rising or the economy is growing, you may be tempted to be more aggressive in your trading decisions, investing more money or taking greater risks. On the contrary, if the news is negative, such as an impending recession or a major drop in the markets, you may feel anxious and decide to sell your positions quickly, even if that goes against your long-term plan. In these cases, the environment pushes you to make decisions based on fear or euphoria of the moment, rather than following a well-thought-out strategy.

Additionally, the physical environment you are in can also influence your decisions. Where you work or trade can affect your level of concentration and your ability to make smart decisions. If you are trading from a noisy place, full of distractions or clutter, you may not be able to think clearly and end up making hasty decisions. On the contrary, if you are in a quiet and organized environment, you are more likely to be able to calmly analyze the situation and make better decisions. Even factors such as the lighting or temperature of your workspace can affect your mood and therefore your financial decisions. An uncomfortable environment can make you feel irritated or anxious, which can lead you to make mistakes that you could have avoided in a more relaxed environment.

Another factor to consider is the influence of culture. Depending on the country or region you live in, culture can play a big role in how you view money and investments. In some cultures, risk is seen as a positive thing, something to be sought out in order to achieve great rewards. In others, risk is perceived as something to be avoided at all costs. These cultural beliefs can influence your trading decisions, making you more or less inclined to take risks. If you live in an environment where financial security is valued above all else, you may be more conservative in your investments, even if circumstances suggest you could be a bit more aggressive. Conversely, if you are in an environment where risk-taking is celebrated, you may feel pressured to invest in more volatile assets, even if that is not the best fit for your situation.

Furthermore, the emotional environment you find yourself in also has a huge impact on your financial decisions. If you are going through a time of stress, anxiety, or even euphoria in your personal life, there is a good chance that this will be reflected in your trading decisions. Trading requires a clear and calm mind, but if you are dealing with personal problems, it can be difficult to maintain the focus and emotional control needed to make good decisions. At such times, it is easy to fall into the trap of making impulsive decisions, either out of fear of losing money or the need to make a quick profit. This is why many successful traders recommend not trading when you are not feeling emotionally balanced, as the emotional environment can cloud your judgment and lead you to make costly mistakes.

It's also important to recognize the influence of the digital environment. Today, we are surrounded by real-time information, via social media, forums, and financial news platforms. This constant information overload can be overwhelming and leave you feeling pressured to act quickly. New expert opinions, analysis, and predictions emerge every day, and it's easy to feel confused or tempted to change your strategy based on what you hear or read online.

However, the key to making good financial decisions is knowing how to filter that information and not let it affect you negatively. A disciplined trader knows that they can't react to every new piece of information, but instead must stick to their plan and rely on their own analysis.

Finally, the global economic environment also plays a key role. Changes in government policies, international conflicts, or economic crises can directly influence the financial markets and, therefore, your trading decisions. Sometimes, fluctuations in the markets are the result of factors that are completely outside of your control, and it is important that you are able to recognize when it is best not to act. Instead of trying to predict the future based on these external events, a successful trader focuses on what he can control, such as his strategy and risk management.

In short, the environment has a significant influence on our financial decisions, especially in trading. Whether it is the social, family, economic, physical or emotional environment, all of these factors can affect the way we make decisions. The key is to be aware of these influences and learn to manage them so as not to let them cloud your judgment. At the end of the day, success in trading is not just about having the best strategy or the best analysis, but about being able to make objective decisions, even when the environment seems to be pushing you in another direction. Learning to recognize and control these external influences is essential to becoming a successful trader and making more balanced and sound financial decisions.

Developing Mental Resilience

Developing mental resilience is one of the most important skills anyone can have in life, and it is especially crucial in the world of trading. Trading is an activity that requires not only technical knowledge and skills, but also mental strength that allows you to remain calm, focused, and confident even when things don't go your way. Mental resilience is what allows you to bounce back from failures, learn from them, and move forward without letting defeats get you down. In this chapter, we are going to explore how you can develop mental resilience and why it is so important to your success in trading and life in general.

First, it is important to understand that trading is an activity that involves high levels of stress and emotions. It is not easy to see how the market goes against your positions or how a decision you thought was right ends in a loss. Many times, these situations can make you feel frustrated, anxious or even doubtful of your abilities. Mental resilience is what will help you handle these difficult times without losing control or making impulsive decisions. Being resilient means accepting that there will be bad days, that you will not always win and that losses are part of the process. But what is most important is how you react to those losses. A mentally resilient trader does not give in to despair or give up. Instead, he analyzes what went wrong, learns from the experience and moves on.

One of the first steps to developing mental resilience is to have a growth mindset. This means that you should view every mistake or failure as an opportunity to learn and improve. If you think of every mistake as a sign that you're not good enough or that you'll never succeed, it will be much harder for you to keep going when you face challenges. But if you can view those mistakes as valuable lessons, you'll be in a better position to improve over time. In trading, this is especially important because you will make mistakes, and it's natural for some trades to not go the way you expected. The key is to learn from each experience and use that knowledge to make better decisions in the future.

Mental resilience also means having control over your emotions. In trading, emotions can be your worst enemies. When things are going well, it's easy to feel elated and confident, but it's also easy to fall into the trap of greed and take more risks than necessary. On the other hand, when things are going badly, it's common to feel fear or despair, which can lead to hasty and miscalculated decisions. Developing mental resilience means learning to manage these emotions and not letting them dictate your decisions. This doesn't mean you should ignore your feelings altogether, but you do need to learn to recognize when your emotions are interfering with your ability to think clearly. A resilient trader is able to stay calm under pressure and stick to their plan, no matter what's happening in the market.

Another key aspect of mental resilience is the ability to maintain confidence in yourself and your strategy, even when you're going through a losing streak. It's very easy to lose confidence when you're faced with a series of failed trades, but it's important to remember that a losing streak doesn't define your ability as a trader. All traders, even the most successful ones, go through tough times when they can't seem to win a single trade. Mental resilience helps you stay confident in those times and keep moving forward with the confidence that things will eventually get better. This doesn't mean you should be stubborn and not change anything; on the contrary, being resilient involves being willing to adjust your approach if necessary, but without losing faith in yourself and your ability to succeed in the long run.

Patience is another key quality in mental resilience. In trading, you won't always see immediate results, and it's important that you are patient and persistent. Mental resilience helps you understand that success in trading doesn't come overnight. It will take time to develop the skills and experience needed to be consistently profitable, and during that time, you're likely to face several obstacles. A mentally resilient trader doesn't give up easily, but is willing to work hard, be patient, and keep going despite challenges. Patience also helps you avoid the temptation to trade impulsively, as you're able to wait for the right opportunities rather than acting only out of a desire for quick profits.

An effective way to build mental resilience is to have a self-care routine. Trading can be very mentally and emotionally demanding, so it's important to take care of yourself both physically and mentally. This includes having good sleeping habits, exercising regularly, and making sure you take breaks when you need to. A burned-out or stressed trader won't be able to make rational decisions and is more prone to making mistakes. Taking care of your personal wellbeing will not only help you become more resilient, but it will also improve your trading performance. Additionally, activities such as meditation or practicing mindfulness can be very useful in helping you manage stress and stay focused.

It's also important to surround yourself with a positive environment that supports your growth process. Mental resilience is strengthened when you have people around you who motivate you, encourage you, and help you see things from a broader perspective. This can be a mentor, a group of traders to share experiences with, or simply friends and family who support you through difficult times. Talking to other people about your challenges and hearing how they have overcome theirs can be a great source of inspiration and will help you stay resilient, even when you face moments of doubt or uncertainty.

Finally, mental resilience requires accepting that trading is a long-term game. It's not about winning today or tomorrow, but about building a career that is sustainable and profitable over time. This means that there will be ups and downs, but as long as you keep learning, improving, and adjusting your strategy, you'll be on the right track. Developing mental resilience will allow you to maintain this long-term vision, without being discouraged by temporary setbacks. Remember that success in trading is not about luck, but about perseverance, discipline, and the ability to bounce back from challenges.

In short, developing mental resilience is critical to success in trading. It involves having a growth mindset, controlling your emotions, staying confident, being patient, and taking care of your personal well-being. The road to success won't always be easy, but with mental resilience, you'll be better prepared to face challenges, learn from them, and move forward with determination. Resilience will not only help you in trading, but also in life in general, as it will allow you to overcome any obstacles that come your way and stay focused on your long-term goals.

Lessons Learned from Major Financial Crises

Financial crises have been a part of economic history for centuries. They are moments when everything seems to fall apart, where panic grips the markets and impulsive decisions become the norm. For traders, each of these crises represents an invaluable lesson on how to manage risk, control emotions and learn from mistakes. In this chapter, we are going to explore some of the great financial crises in history and the lessons we can draw from them. These lessons are not only useful for traders, but also for anyone who wants to understand how markets work and how to survive times of turbulence.

One of the most remembered crises is the Great Depression of 1929. This economic collapse affected not only the United States, but also much of the world. It all started with the stock market crash in October of that year, causing thousands of investors to lose their fortunes overnight. The most important lesson we can learn from this event is the importance of not getting carried away by market euphoria. In the years leading up to the crash, the stock market had experienced exponential growth, leading many to invest without considering the risk. Unmeasured optimism blinded investors, who believed that prices would continue to rise indefinitely. However, the market eventually corrected itself and panic took hold. This teaches us that although the market may seem to be constantly on the rise, it is always necessary to have a solid strategy and not blindly trust that prices will continue to rise forever.

Another financial crisis that left important lessons was the dot-com bubble in 2000. At that time, the rise of technology companies led to an investment rush in the sector. Anything related to the internet seemed like a safe bet, and many investors invested in shares of companies that were not even generating real profits. Just like in the Great Depression, the lesson here is that market euphoria can be dangerous. In the world of trading, it is very easy to get carried away by trends and jump on the fad of the moment, but it is crucial to remember that not every company, sector or asset is a solid investment just because it is booming. Many of the companies in the dot-com bubble did not survive the market crash, and those who invested in them without properly researching or considering the risks lost large sums of money. The key is to always do your own research and not base your decisions solely on what is trendy.

A similar lesson can be drawn from the 2008 financial crisis, when the US housing market collapsed and took global financial markets with it. This event showed how problems in a seemingly stable sector, such as the housing market, can trigger a domino effect that affects the entire economy. One of the most important lessons from this crisis is the need to understand the hidden risks in the markets. In the case of the 2008 crisis, many investors did not understand the complexity of the financial products they were purchasing, such as mortgage-backed securities. The lack of transparency in these products made it difficult for many to assess the actual risk they were exposed to. As a trader, it is critical that you always understand what you are investing in and are aware of the risks involved. If something seems too complicated or confusing, it is best to avoid it until you have a full understanding of how it works.

Another key lesson from the 2008 crisis is the importance of risk management. During the housing bubble, many investors and banks took on excessive risks, trusting that house prices would continue to rise indefinitely. When prices began to fall, a crisis of epic proportions ensued. This situation highlights the importance of not over-leveraging – that is, not borrowing more money than you can realistically handle in case the market does not behave as you expected. In trading, the use of leverage can be a powerful tool, but it can also be extremely dangerous if not used carefully. Proper risk management, including controlling how much you are willing to lose on a trade, is critical to surviving periods of high volatility.

The COVID-19 pandemic in 2020 also brought with it a global economic crisis that affected markets in unpredictable ways. Within weeks, stock markets around the world suffered drastic declines as investors reacted to the impact of the pandemic. However, what is interesting about this crisis is that it also showed how quickly markets can recover. Despite the initial panic, markets recovered in record time, driven in large part by economic stimulus from governments and central banks. One of the lessons of this crisis is that while panic can grip markets in times of uncertainty, it is also important not to lose sight of the bigger picture. Many investors who sold at the bottom of the crisis missed the opportunity to benefit from the recovery that came after. This situation teaches us that in times of high volatility, it is important to stay calm, stick to your trading plan, and not make impulsive decisions based on fear.

Every financial crisis reminds us that markets are volatile and there will always be periods of uncertainty. As a trader, it is essential to learn to accept this reality and develop a mindset that will allow you to survive the ups and downs of the market. Crises are not the end of the world, although they may seem that way at the time. In fact, they often represent opportunities for those who are prepared and know how to handle them. Lessons learned from past crises teach us the importance of patience, risk management, emotional control, and careful research. If you can apply these lessons to your own trading, you will be better prepared to deal with any crises that may arise in the future.

Finally, it is important to remember that crises are not only economic, but also emotional. The pressure and stress they create can affect your mental health and decision-making. That is why one of the most valuable lessons from any crisis is to learn how to take care of yourself. Staying calm, having a positive mindset, and being resilient will help you get through even the toughest times in trading and in life. Crises are inevitable, but with the right lessons, you can not only survive them, but also come out stronger from them.

The Path from Novice to Expert Trader

The path a trader takes from novice to expert is full of challenges, learnings, and many experiences that shape the way they operate in the markets. At first, everything seems new and sometimes overwhelming. There is a lot of information to learn, terms that seem complex, and strategies that sound too technical. However, over time, each of these elements begins to make sense, and what once seemed complicated becomes clearer. A trader's journey is a process that requires time, patience, and above all, the willingness to make mistakes and learn from them.

When a trader starts out, they often do so with high expectations. It's easy to believe that trading is a quick path to riches, influenced by success stories circulating on the internet or social media. Many newbies come in thinking that within a few months they will be able to generate significant income and change their life. However, the reality is very different. Trading is not a get-rich-quick scheme. Instead, it is a skill that is developed with practice, patience, and a lot of discipline. Expert traders know that consistent profits don't come overnight, and part of the learning process is adjusting those initial expectations to be more realistic.

The first big hurdle for newbies is often controlling emotions. At first, fear and greed play a huge role in their decisions. It is common that after a first loss, a newbie trader panics and closes a trade early or, on the contrary, holds a position too long waiting for the market to change direction. Emotions are one of the main reasons why newbie traders tend to lose money in their early stages. The lesson here is that learning to control emotions is key to moving forward on the path to success. Expert traders do not let fear or greed influence their decisions; instead, they stick to their trading plan and trust their analysis.

Another important aspect of this journey is continued education. At first, a novice trader will often spend time reading books, watching videos, and following other more experienced traders to learn the basics. This is a critical stage, as the information absorbed at this point will be the foundation on which future knowledge will be built. However, learning does not end here. An expert trader knows that the market is constantly changing, and therefore, it is necessary to keep learning and adapting. As he progresses in his career, a trader continues to study new strategies, techniques, and adapt to market trends. The difference between a novice trader and an expert trader lies in the ability to keep learning and improving over time.

In this process, making mistakes is inevitable. Every trader, regardless of their level of experience, has experienced losing moments. However, what differentiates a novice from an expert is how they handle those mistakes. A novice trader may feel discouraged after a loss and may decide to give up or change their strategy immediately, without stopping to analyze what went wrong. On the other hand, an expert trader sees losses as an opportunity to learn. They evaluate what mistakes they made, adjust their plan, and move on. Losses should not be seen as failures, but as valuable lessons that bring you closer to mastery. Every trade, winning or losing, is an opportunity to improve.

Once a beginner trader starts to gain more confidence, it is common for them to experience a stage of overconfidence or arrogance. After making some profits, it is easy to fall into the trap of thinking that success is guaranteed. This can lead to making hasty or risky decisions, often resulting in unexpected losses. At this point, the trader begins to learn the importance of humility. No matter how many times you have been successful in the past, the market can always surprise you, and an expert trader knows this. Part of personal growth on this path is learning to stay calm and not get carried away by euphoria after a few wins.

Additionally, as a trader becomes more skilled, they learn the importance of having a solid strategy. In the beginning, it's common for newbies to jump from strategy to strategy, trying different approaches and hoping to find "the magic formula." However, expert traders know that there is no such thing. Instead of searching for the perfect system, they focus on developing a strategy that works for them, one that is aligned with their trading style, risk tolerance, and personal goals. Beyond strategies, they also learn to trust their own skills and analysis, rather than blindly following the opinions of others.

Discipline also plays a crucial role on the path to success. Expert traders understand that long-term success does not depend on making big profits quickly, but on maintaining consistency over time. This means following the trading plan without deviating, even when emotions try to interfere. A novice trader may be tempted to enter or exit a trade early, or risk more than they should. However, an experienced trader knows that discipline is key to avoiding costly mistakes and maintaining a focused mindset.

Finally, one aspect that is often underestimated in the trading path is personal balance. Trading can be mentally exhausting, especially in the early years. A novice trader can spend hours in front of the screen, analyzing charts and looking for the next opportunity. Over time, he or she realizes that balance is essential. Expert traders know that in order to be successful, it is also necessary to take care of mental and physical health. This involves taking breaks, disconnecting from the market, and having a balanced life outside of trading. Success is not only measured in terms of profits, but also in quality of life and personal well-being.

The road from a novice to an expert trader is long and, in many cases, full of obstacles. However, with each step taken, the trader becomes wiser, more disciplined, and more aware of how to navigate the markets. There are no shortcuts on this journey, but those who persevere and are willing to learn from their mistakes, constantly educate themselves, and maintain emotional control will find that, over time, trading success is an attainable reality.

Trading and Personal Life

Trading can be an all-consuming activity, where financial markets, charts, and economic news become a fundamental part of your daily routine. However, it is also important to remember that while trading can be exciting and demanding, it should not completely take over your personal life. One of the biggest challenges for those who trade, whether as a full-time or part-time activity, is finding a work-life balance. When trading becomes a top priority, it can take a toll on relationships, health, and overall happiness.

One of the first things a trader needs to be clear about is the need to set boundaries. It's easy to fall into the trap of always keeping an eye on the market, especially when trading in markets that operate 24 hours a day, such as the currency or cryptocurrency markets. The constant movement of prices and the opportunities that can arise at any time can generate anxiety and a sense of urgency to always be connected. However, if a trader does not set clear schedules for working and disconnecting, trading can invade all areas of their life. This can lead to neglecting health, family relationships, or even hobbies and activities that they previously enjoyed.

In addition to setting schedules, it is also essential for traders to learn how to mentally switch off when they are not trading. It is one thing to physically step away from the screen, but quite another to stop thinking about the market. Many novice traders obsess over their decisions, mentally reviewing the trades they made or plan to make the next day. This attitude is not only exhausting, but can also generate unnecessary stress. Switching off means allowing the mind to rest, to focus on other activities that have nothing to do with trading. In the end, this not only benefits personal life, but also performance in the markets, as a rested mind is much more efficient when making decisions.

Another important aspect of trading-life balance is the emotional impact it can have. Trading, by its nature, involves taking risks and sometimes losses. These losses, if not managed correctly, can lead to frustration, anxiety or even feelings of failure. It is essential for traders to know how to separate their personal identity from their results in the market. Having a losing trade does not mean that the trader has failed as a person, and it is essential that this mentality does not carry over into personal life. When a trader allows their losses to affect their emotional state and, in turn, their interaction with others, the imbalance becomes evident. The key is to maintain a professional attitude towards trading, understanding that it is part of a broader process, but that it does not define who you are outside the markets.

Support from family and friends is crucial to maintaining a healthy balance. Often, traders work from home, which can make it difficult for their loved ones to fully understand what their job entails. It is common for some family members to think that because they are at home, the trader is available at all times or that their activity is not "as serious." Explaining the commitment that trading requires can help improve understanding and mutual respect for personal time and spaces. At the same time, it is important for the trader to also understand that although trading is a significant part of their life, it should not replace quality time with loved ones.

One of the big risks of trading is that when things go wrong in the market, it can be tempting to work longer hours or constantly check charts for a quick fix. However, this is rarely productive. In fact, when a trader is emotionally affected, they are more likely to make impulsive or reckless decisions, which can make the situation worse. At these times, it is most important to take a step back, breathe, and focus on other areas of life. Going for a walk, spending time with family, or engaging in a relaxing activity can help clear your mind and return to the market with a refreshed perspective.

It is also vital for traders to stay physically active. Trading is an activity that is, more often than not, done by sitting in front of a computer for long hours. Lack of physical exercise not only affects physical health, but also mental health. Exercise is proven to help reduce stress, improve concentration, and promote a positive mood. Making time for physical activity, even if it is just a few minutes of walking a day, can have a significant impact on a trader's ability to handle market pressures and maintain a balanced personal life.

Finally, it is important for a trader to have hobbies and activities outside of the market. Having diverse interests is key to maintaining a balanced life. It can be reading a good book, playing a sport, learning a new skill, or simply spending time with friends. These activities not only help to relax, but also provide a broader perspective on life. By having other areas that bring happiness and satisfaction, trading is no longer the only factor that determines emotional well-being. It is easier to handle losses or difficult days in the market when you have a life rich in other aspects.

Trading can be a very fulfilling career, but it is also an activity that requires a strong mindset and a disciplined approach. Achieving a balance between trading and personal life is a challenge that many traders face, but it is essential for long-term success. Maintaining that balance will not only improve a trader's quality of life, but it will also make them more effective at their job, as a clear and balanced mind will always make better decisions. Trading is just one part of life, and at the end of the day, what really matters are relationships, health, and overall well-being. Learning to balance these aspects is what will allow you to fully enjoy both worlds.

www.ingramcontent.com/pod-product-compliance
Lightning Source LLC
Chambersburg PA
CBHW051852130726
47987CB00002B/800